Perfectly Imperfect

By: Fatimata Cham

Copyright © 2019 by Fatimata Cham.

All rights reserved, including the right to reproduce this book or portions thereof in any form whatsoever. For more information address The Literary Revolutionary, YBF Publishing LLC. PO Box 361526 Decatur, GA 30036

ISBN #: 978-1-950279-13-5

Edited by: Capital J
Editor-in-Chief: Nia Sade Akinyemi, The Literary Revolutionary
Cover Design by: Opeyemi Ikuborije Olorunfemi

Manufactured in the United States of America

For information regarding special discounts for bulk purchases, please contact The Literary Revolutionary Special Sales Team at 470-396-0660 or support@theliteraryrevolutionary.com

Follow Fatimata!
Instagram: @fatimata_cham

This book is dedicated to my parents, my family and friends for constantly believing in me, and for people of color who want to become writers.

Acknowledgements

Writing a book is a beautiful experience and harder than I thought it would be. First and foremost, I would like to thank Allah s.w.t. for giving me this opportunity. I would like to thank my mother for always believing in me, my father for giving me the tools at a very young age to help me become the writer I am today. I would like to also thank my publisher Nia for all her hard work in ensuring that Black authors are recognized and heard. I would lastly like to thank my peers and my fellow writers. Never stop believing in yourself and the power that words have.

Oh Sad Brown Girl

Oh sad brown girl

Don't you cry

They want your lips

Your curves

But not your beautiful melanin

Oh sad brown girl

It's okay

Your tears run through the Nile river

For you come from a line of queens

Who ran kingdoms for ages

Oh sad brown girl

Lift your head up high

For you have written stories

That they love to hear so much

Oh sad brown girl

Don't you cry

Look in the mirror clearly

Their lies no imperfection

For you are a creation of God

Oh sad brown girl

There's a reason why they itch to touch

Your beautiful curly hair

Oh sad brown girl

You are magnificent

Walk with grace

Walk with light

Oh sad brown girl

I love you

In the Little Nook of Books

In the little nook of books

There you'll find her

In the opening of the window

Whilst the sun is setting

Leaves changing color

There you'll find her

In the swaying of the trees

In each snowflake falling

In the beating of a broken child's heart

There you'll find her

At the sound of a mother's scream

While giving birth to La Vie

There you'll find her

When he gets his first report card

When he gets his first kiss

When he finds love

When he gets married

Has children

Grows old

Sitting in his rocking chair

Reading a book

In a little nook

There you'll find her

She isn't a human being

She isn't me

Nor is she an alien

She isn't a shooting star

Or one of the planets orbiting the sun

She isn't a particle

Floating, invisible

She isn't my friend

She's you

A wonder

200 Pages to Fill

Words gliding across the page

Books stacked high in the corner

I am perplexed

At how I ended up like this

I drum my fingers

Across the table

Still pondering

On what I should write in this

black and white composition notebook

Pacing around the house

I hear the Adhan

Calling me to prayer

But I know

There's still writing to be done

But nonetheless

I place my head on the prayer mat

In my room I am surrounded by white walls

Covered in my little brothers scribble

He could be Picasso one day

His tiny little fingers

Big brown eyes

Have yet to see the world

We all try to often to run away from

21st Century Activist

What is a true activist

I ask this question all the time

Am I an activist

Does liking this on Facebook

And Instagram make me a

So called activist

Does sitting home on my couch

And writing with my pen make me an activist

I've come to realize that in the world

The definition of an activist has changed

Over time

But are we activist

When those students from Little Rock,

Stood in front of the school

And had to push through a mob of people

Just to get an education

Were they activists?

When Martin Luther King Jr.

Led a march to Washington

Were they activists?

When Prophet Muhammad (SAW)

Went to Makkah to Medina

For the sake of his religion a true sign of activism

Are we all activist or is it all in our mind

Not until we die for what we believe are we ever

Truly activist

Not until we stop liking and retweeting and

Start doing are we ever truly ever activist

I am not activist but another human being

With goals and writing to change the world we live in today

Dear Whom It May Concern

I was wondering when you would inform me about this

About the broken education system

About the broken justice system

About our broken gun laws

About America

Home of the Brave

Home of the red, white, and blue

About our president

Dear whom may concern,

I was wondering when you began to realize that it was too late

Dear whom may concern

I was wondering when war would in end in Afghanistan

I was wondering when the war in Syria would end

Dear whom may concern

I was wondering when you finally pop the bubble

The bubble that we are the top country

That we are doing just fine

Dear whom may concern,

I was wondering when you would let me vote

Dear whom may concern,

While I was wondering

I pondered on what I could do about it

So, I wrote this poem

Dear whom it may concern

Are you concerned or are you scared?

Are you scared about the thousands of teens that will march for our lives on Saturday

Are you scared about losing our vote?

Well you should be

Because we are tired of the handcuffs that you have put on

Uncuff us and let our voices ring until you can't hear no more

Symphony

An orange leaf

Fallen off on a Sunday morning

One that nobody picks up

It lies there for days at a time

But I do

It's special

It's not just orange but it's bright

It's beautiful and it's one that

I place in my scrapbook

For safekeeping

I call it

Symphony

Boxes

Even in the darkest of moments

Life wasn't so dull anymore

It became this box

Full of voices of the unknown

Chemo

Life was

This inanimate object

She couldn't touch

And she never would

For some reason

God chose her

The disease kept spreading like wildfire

And her eyes were bloodshot red

After every round of chemo

She became hopeless

It was this ongoing

Perpetuating cycle

She always looked up to the sky

And wondered

If she was strong enough

If life would keep her from falling

For some reason

It didn't

She ended up falling

But she had to find a way to climb

Back up the ladder

An unknown force was making her stronger

She would never know what it was

But after the last rotund of chemo

When the doctor told her it

Would be the last time

The sun came out and

It shined right on her

Left cheek

Lie

In the eyes of people

I know

There's a web lies

They continue to weave

But the web is invisible

I wish I knew why

There's a hidden darkness

In the eyes of the people

I know

I hate them

Because they lie

Your Story

Life is a series of colors

Pick your color

Pick up a paintbrush

And paint your story

12 Truths and a Lie

It's hidden beneath her scarf

It's the ticking time bomb

The foreign state

Of sadness

Cold air

Blossoming between her shoulders

She is

The seed

That you forgot to nurture

The loud noise

She struggles to see herself

Devouring your sadness

Into the depths of her despair

Lies

They say it's not good to lie

But when will we all stop lying?

We live in a society

Where we tell everybody to be themselves

Yet we're so quick to judge based on what a person is wearing

We live, sleep, eat, breathe

Lies

It's okay to be who you are

Until you're breaking the latest fashion trend

Until your speaking a language that's not yours

Until you step out of your comfort zone

We keep telling

White **lies**

We tell everybody to speak the truth

Yet we don't want to hear it

We live, sleep, eat, breath

Lies

Well since I'm writing this poem

Aren't I a liar too

Because I'm not courageous enough to

Tell it to your face

So instead I use art as a way to communicate

The **lies**

We are all liars

But how can we stop

When where so quick

To succumb to pressure

We live

Lies

It's time we stop.

Fall

Fall is coming

The leaves are changing color

Why can't She too?

Why can't she

Blend in

Until all the fallen leaves

Have caressed every square inch of

Her broken body

She's become numb

From the temperature dropping

Fall is coming

The leaves are changing color

Why can't her life change too?

Pretend

I *pretend*

To color in my coloring book

I *pretend* to play

Hide and seek

I run in circles

Because he said it was okay

I *pretend*

He tells me to count to 3

So that it will be over

I *pretend* to smile

I *pretend*

So that he won't hurt me

He tells me loves me

I *pretend*

So that I believe it

But I don't wanna pretend anymore

So, I uncuff myself from him

And fly away

I don't look back

I become stronger

So that

I no longer *pretend*

Beauty

Beauty is something she never

Talks about

It's the devil that haunts her in her sleep

Beauty is the pen

That she twiddled in between her

Little fingers she tries to write with

But her words become

Nothing but scribbles on a paper

That she paints on her paper

Not the physical attributes

Not her eyes nor her nose

It's not her life

Beauty is the line between

Hate and love

It's Her

Inner demon

Don't call me beautiful she says

Don't because my name is not Beauty

It's Beast

Because Beast

Was not pretty

Beast was compassion

Raw anger

And anything but extraordinary

A Child

I am the child of

Immigrants

Who crosses oceans do get to this country

I am the child

Of dreamers who looked up at the sky

And painted their dreams

I am the child of

A construction worker

Who works day and night to make sure I have what I need

I am the child

Of a nurse

Who tries her best to make sure her patients are okay

I am the child of

Muslim immigrants

Who pray to Allah s.w.t.

I am the child of an African women and African man

Who left everything behind to come here

I am the child of Americans.

I am the child of red white and blue

I am the child

Who writes tirelessly so that people can hear my parents voice

I am the child

Who marches, advocates and will not rest until inequality is nothing but a distant memory

I am a child

But in this great nation

With all the inequality, police brutality,

It's seems to me that being a child

Is nothing but a fairytale

No more games at recess or

Thinking about fairytales

You see right in America

Students can't sit in a classroom without having to worry about

Someone coming to school with a gun

We can't sit in a classroom and posing our dreams in the white walls

But that is why we must continue to fight

Because we are the children of dreamers,

Immigrants, hard workers and love.

The Heart

At the heart of America

Lies the child

Who has yet to discover her untapped

Potential

At the heart of America

Lies racism and inequality

At the heart of America

Lies me

Though I am unsure of what life holds

I have seen the very dream

That lies within all of us

The ability to love and care for each other

The ability to not let someone's

Appearance

Determine what you think of them

At the heart of America

There's me

There's you

And anyone who dreams of becoming

NZ

50 lives lost

In a place of worship

"Hello Brother"

What do you think of them now

Innocent lives lost

Praying

Children died

Mothers died

A father died

Yet you let the hate consume your very soul

I am Muslim

They are Muslim

And we are dying

But no one seems to care

No one seems to listen

We are dying in Syria

We are dying in Burma

We are dying in Afghanistan

We are dying

We are dying

Numb

How many more tears do we have to cry

Before you get it

How many more lives have to end

Before you get it

The news stories

Flash across my screen

My body is numb

From the pain in my heart

You ask me the same questions

We give you the answers

Hands up don't shoot

You expect us to stay calm

When you've got a loaded gun

Pointed at us

Hand up don't shoot

You tell us to stay in school

Yet the curriculum wasn't made for us

We don't see ourselves in your whitewashed history

But I consider myself one of the lucky

Ones

Because I can still speak in my native tongue

Kunta Kinte remember his name

Remember their names

Because they will forget

You tell me to be brave, to be strong

But every time I walk into a classroom

I can't stand it

Being the only one

How many more years do we need to cry

Before our voices stop getting drowned out

Me

She wrote her dreams down on this

Crumpled up piece of paper

She glanced down

As her fingers started to quake

She glanced back

Only to find a window

With a quarter sized hole in it

Glass shards lay on the floor

She could see her reflection through them

Her father locked up behind bars

She wrote her dreams on this

Crumpled up piece of paper

No one dared to acknowledge her existence

She slowly began to fade away into the background

Each day

She withered away

And when her mother walked in

It was already too late

She swept away those shards of glass

But little did she know

Those shards of glass where her daughter

The daughter she couldn't "fix"

This is what happens when no one listens

My Name

"Can you shorten your name?"

I guess my name is too hard to pronounce

On the white man's tongue

Fatimata

I've lived my life trying to confine to you

Trying to make sure you were comfortable enough

Fatimata

Can you shorten your name?

Why

Because it's not normal

It's not beautiful enough for you

It is not grand enough for you

Fatimata

Can you shorten your name?

Next time my answer will be

No, my name is Fatimata

I am a writer

A learner

A listener

I am a child

A daughter

Whose parents crossed oceans to come here

Fatimata is my name

Remember it

News

We've become numb

Daily news

Good Morning America

But mornings aren't good anymore

You see living in Gen Z

We learned to speak up

Before we learned to ride our bikes

We learned to duck under tables

Before we learned our ABC's

We've become numb

Another one dead

Another child gone

Another light left to burn out

Good morning America

But mornings aren't good anymore

Another government shutdown

People out of jobs

Good morning America

Good night I've become numb

A Message

Live your dreams

Learn to fly

Spread your wings

Do not cry

Live your dreams

Do not cry

Spread your wings

Beautiful Butterfly

Part II

I sit here and try to write but it comes up as a blank. You would think that it would be easy to write about something like this but it's not because the truth is there are a million black and Muslim girls in America and I'm just one of them. How can I speak for all when I can't even speak for myself sometimes?

Here's my first experience.

I was in the second grade. Sitting at a table. I look around the room and there's only one of me. I feel lost and try so hard to belong, but it doesn't work. They keep asking me the same question over and over again... "Why do you wear that on your head?" and I draw a blank.

I realize I do not know how to answer it. Then it happens. Someone pulled off my hijab. I just remember sitting there and time froze. Everything around me became still. The only noise I could hear was the laughter and sound of children who are laughing at my curly, kinky hair. The hair that has been embedded in my genes. The hair that makes me African American. They took away something that made me feel protected...my hijab. After that day the questions never came up again.

My second experience but not my last. At a March for Equal Rights. In a crowd of 8,000 people. I was standing with my bright red coat on. I felt protected. We were all rejoicing. Me and my friends adults and children alike. My sign had a heart symbol and a smiley face because love is the only way right. I was happy and I had the biggest smile because no one could take that away from me...Then he came. The man with the yellow shirt. He approached me. And told me he would buy me a first-class ticket back to Africa. He told me I didn't belong. This wasn't my country. Something I have been told all my life. My mind froze. I felt so weak. I walked away. I didn't yell at him. I followed my heart and it told me to walk away. I couldn't help but believe that it was true. Sitting in the comfort of strangers who showed me love and kindness. I learned that while I was fighting the battle inside that I was not alone. It was the actions of a stranger that made it all worthwhile. I didn't know her name, but she told me I was better than that. I thought my world was falling apart, my heart was breaking at the seams. I wanted to crawl into a whole and never come out. Everyone has a story.

This is just one part of mine. Whether you see a Muslim woman gracing the cover of teen vogue and vogue Arabia or a Muslim woman fencing at the Olympics. Whether you see her sitting quietly in the corner or hear her voice filling up the room when you walk in. Just know that just because she chooses to wear the niqab or chooses to wear the hijab or chooses to not wear it, that it does not make her any less of a Muslim then the person sitting next to her. I have had to face many struggles because many people believe that because I am a hijabi I am oppressed but I choose to get up in the morning and wrap this beautiful scarf on my head and I wear it proudly. I am in this fight to show that that being a feminist or a hijabi or someone who is an activist can't stop you from accomplishing your goals. Matter-of-a-fact, I will be the first in my family to attend a four-year college and certainly will not be the last.

Perfectly Imperfect

I am perfectly imperfect

I have my flaws

I am composed of particles

I am Gambian

I am American

I am Fatimata

You are human

You have your flaws

But what are we without them

You are perfectly Imperfect

About The Author

Fatimata was born and raised in the Bronx, New York. She is a recent high school graduate and new student attending Lafayette College. Fatimata is a member of Harvard University's *Making Caring Common* Youth Advisory Board. Since 2015, she has been a member of the Junior Academy that works alongside The New York Academy of the Sciences to help build the world's next leaders. Fatimata has served as the Community Service Club President of her high school, helping to engage her school, along with some of her peers, in discussion involving diversity and inclusion. She was chosen among many applicants to become a delegate to the United

Nations at their Youth Assembly and is also a Girl Up teen advisor to the United Nations Foundation.

Fatimata is an avid reader, writer, and blogger. In her free time, she writes poetry and shares it with her peers. She writes for the Muslim Youth Musings and Miss Heard Media blogs, respectively. Both blogs engage her peers in discussion surrounding being a young Muslim teen and being a girl in America. Fatimata is the recipient of The Samuel Robinson II Community Service Award for the many hours she contributes to community service in her free time. Fatimata is compassionate and has committed to the betterment of the people that surround her.

She is the founder of her own organization called *Leaders of the Future*. She created this organization in hopes of providing space where teens from around the country can brainstorm and create discussion around climate change. Fatimata is a firm believer that if we can create spaces where teens are allowed to discuss some of the world's problems, we are creating the leaders of today.

In the world we live in today there are many pressing issues ranging from mass shootings, to climate change, and the systematic abuse and oppression of minority groups. This book of poetry talks about beauty standards, issues faced by people in my community, and issues I see our world facing today. Poetry is truly a lens we can use to change the world.

www.ingramcontent.com/pod-product-compliance
Lightning Source LLC
Chambersburg PA
CBHW071800040426
42446CB00012B/2646